For Hannah, loved by Jesus
D. D. M.

For John Knapp and Paul Herpich,
cherished friends in Christ
D. C.

A Tree for Christmas

Written by Dandi Daley Mackall

Illustrated by Dominic Catalano

CONCORDIA PUBLISHING HOUSE • SAINT LOUIS

Was there wood in the manger that held our Lord?

Did His tiny fingers touch the smooth, worn board?

Was a tree cut down for the Child adored?

We needed a tree for Christmas.

As a boy, did Jesus, in His father's shop,

Learn to build with cedars and a *chop, chop, chop*?

Did He hammer boards until He had to stop?

We needed a tree for Christmas.

Once, a man so short that he could not see,

Climbed a tall, tall branch of a sycamore tree.

Jesus called, "Zacchaeus, come and follow Me!"

We needed a tree for Jesus.

There was wood in the boat in a storm at sea,

When they cried to the Man from Galilee.

Then the storm grew calm, and the boat sailed free.

We needed a tree for Jesus.

When He said, "Be fruitful. Live abundantly—"

Or He told a parable of how life should be—

When He taught a lesson from a bare fig tree ...

We needed a tree for Jesus.

Did the tree leaves rustle as a soft breeze blew,

When He taught, "God's Spirit comes to live in you,

Like the wind—invisible, but still so true"?

We needed a tree for Jesus.

Jesus rode in triumph as the Son God gave,

For He loved the people that He came to save.

When they cut down branches they could lift and wave ...

We needed a tree for Jesus.

In the Upper Room, they prepared to dine.

There was wood in the table where they placed the wine.

"For I bring you forgiveness with this Gift of Mine."

We needed a tree for Jesus.

Was there wood in the cross that held our Lord?

Did His bruised, worn fingers touch the splintered board?

Was a tree cut down for the Christ adored?

We needed a tree for Jesus.

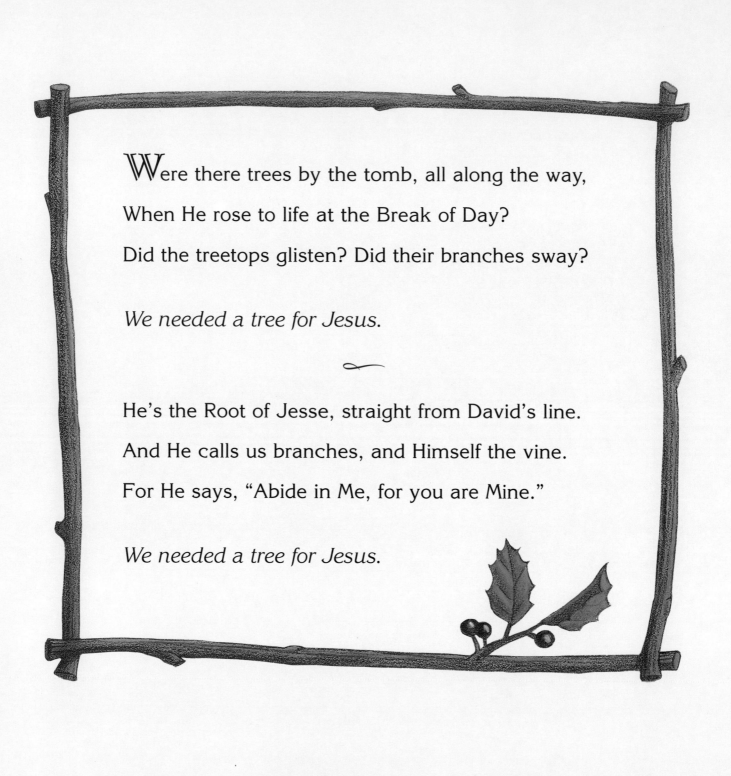

Were there trees by the tomb, all along the way,

When He rose to life at the Break of Day?

Did the treetops glisten? Did their branches sway?

We needed a tree for Jesus.

He's the Root of Jesse, straight from David's line.

And He calls us branches, and Himself the vine.

For He says, "Abide in Me, for you are Mine."

We needed a tree for Jesus.

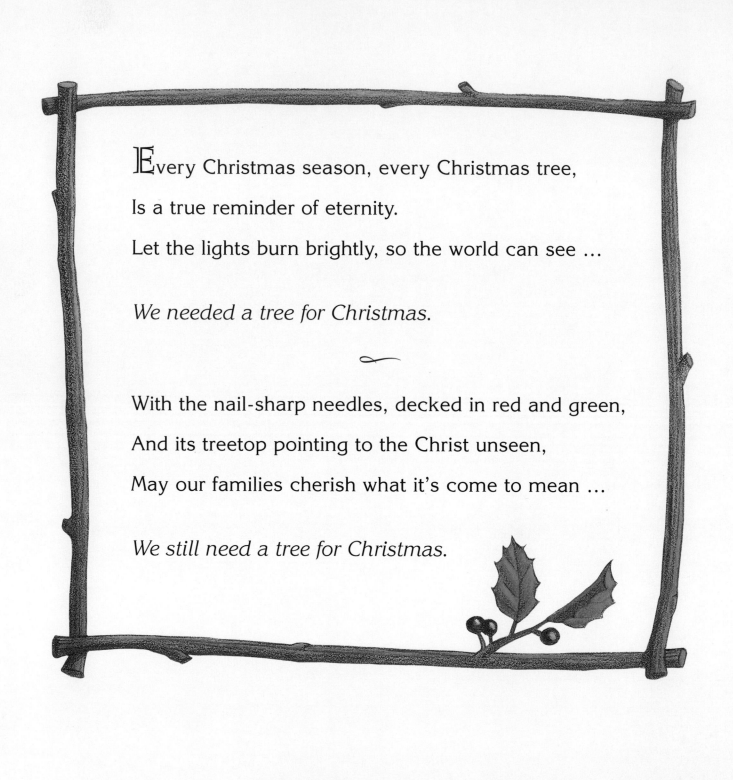

Every Christmas season, every Christmas tree,

Is a true reminder of eternity.

Let the lights burn brightly, so the world can see ...

We needed a tree for Christmas.

With the nail-sharp needles, decked in red and green,

And its treetop pointing to the Christ unseen,

May our families cherish what it's come to mean ...

We still need a tree for Christmas.

Published by Concordia Publishing House
3558 S. Jefferson Avenue
St. Louis, MO 63118-3968